Declutter

50 Steps To Help You Stop
And Start Organizing Your Home Life, Work Life
And Personal Life Immediately

By David Spencer

Copyright @2018 David Spencer

All rights reserved. No part of this book may be reproduced in any form or by any means without permission in writing from the publisher, .

If you like my book, please leave a positive review on Amazon. I would appreciate it a lot. Thanks! This is the link:

Leave your review here. Thank you!

Contents

Introduction 4

Tips 1-7 6

Tips 8-14 14

Tips 15-21 20

Tips 22-28 28

Tips 29-36 36

Tips 37-43 43

Tips 44-50 51

Conclusion 58

Introduction

I must get my office and individual life sorted out! When did you last utter these words? Is it accurate to say that it was the point at which you perceived that you're truly suffocating under mounds of paper? Maybe it was the point at which you got a look of the tremendous pile of clothes that you can never appear to get up to speed with. Perhaps it was the point at which you took a gander at all of the clutter in your kitchen, cellar, bedroom, carport, and wherever else. You may have even contemplated hurling everything out the window! Is it safe to say that it was the point at which you desperately needed to hunt down those missing concert tickets? It might have been the point at which you missed that important arrangement. Or on the other hand when that due date for a project sneaked up on you. Maybe it was the point at which you thought that you had enough To Do's on your list to last you a life time. Is it safe to say that it was the point at which you critically looked for that missing clients file?

Or then again much more dreadful, it may have happened when you decided you had no time left for yourself, your other half, your associates, that required vacation and essentially, everything in life that you want to do.

You're not the only one. Those words have been communicated over and over by a great many people everywhere throughout the world. Confusion may really trap you into carrying on with an existence loaded with pressure, disappointment and uproar. It might deny you of the valuable time you should spend making the most of your life. By eliminating all of this un-organization, you might be able to carry on with the kind of life you've generally longed for. You should be organized!

Tips 1-7

In case you're tired of living in a life of messiness and that you can't ever discover what you require when you require it, you've come to the perfect place. This book will help you to get your life composed, with extra special care. Actually, you can start right now.

What are the most confusing aspects of your life? The ones that makes you completely insane? Your storage room? Your home office? The children's room? You can take the very first steps by getting everything in order by imagining what it is you want.

Get A Vision

1. Ascertain your objectives.

Before you start anything, find out its objective. In the event that you don't know where you're going, by what method will you want to get there? Set scaled down objectives and strengthen yourself for victories.

Try not to acknowledge more than you may deal with too early, especially if your objective is something outside of your insight or present cabability. It's not very hard to have your mood put down when you perceive that your objective of running 3 miles daily has dwindled following 2 weeks since you can't move beyond one mile daily. Unless you've been a dynamic athelete, it's smarter to start moderate and work your way up. When you start little and set small objectives for yourself, you're significantly more liable to succeed.

You just started a new job as a business assistant and have an objective of getting to be deals director in a half year. That is in all likelihood not going to happen, and you're setting yourself up for frustration. Set objectives that are getable by surveying reality of the circumstance and learning. This is especially essential when defining objectives where another person assumes a significant part in whether you achieve your goals, similar to your supervisor or boss. It's extraordinary to aim high, however sometimes you can't achieve your objective if its too far out of reach realistically.

2. Unclutter your work area.

An uncluttered work area eradicates un-needed diversions and helps keep your mind on errands that require quick consideration. Keep just the particulars around your work area that are needed in your present tasks.

Clear the PC work area of paper. Store away a large portion of the material beyond anyone's ability to see in filing cabinets and folders. Place a cheat sheet on an adjacent board or somewhere close by for information that must be immediately gotten to, similar to telephone numbers and non-private account numbers; this will lessen the measure of paper on the work area. Keep the number of pens and pencils on the work area to a minimum and keep just the ones you use all the time. Put most pens and pencils conveniently away in a cabinet.

3. Do not put trust in that memory of yours.

You risk giving endeavors a chance to escape. The most helpful approach to always remember an arrangement, a due date or a specific event, is to keep a record of it, simply write it down.

An arrangement book encourages you to compose your meetings adequately. It empowers you to organize exercises as indicated by their significance, when they must be proficient, and to prepare. For instance, on the off chance that you know the correct date of a critical gathering seven days previously, you can set aside time to plan for it all the more successfully.

4.   Consolidate activities.

Instead of starting and halting at various levels of action, you'll spare time by doing the majority of your phone calls at the same time, dealing with every one of your errands at one time, and so on.

Combine the cooking by making a batch and then putting them in the freezer, and the n make the easier dinners daily that only take a fraction of the time. Sort out the shopping so you just go once per week, once every 10 days, or even once every fortnight.

5.   Clear out your records.

Before you experience the cost of purchasing more file organizers, envelopes, and so on, set aside the opportunity to cleanse all unneeded materials.

Isolate the papers that are really essential like, bills and receipts that you have to keep for important purposes, statements and so forth.

6.   Utilize one big calendar.

The greatest mistake people make while using calendars is to keep more than one. Keep individual, work and family events on one schedule. It will wipe out booking clashes. Keep in mind, 'the man who wears two watches, never knows the opportune time.'

With the worlds busy schedules and everything that goes on from day to day, it would be wise to run your email, calendars and updates in a single component.

Using an online timetable component will guarantee that you'll never miss an engagement since you forgot about time surfing the Web.

7. Cut down telephone time.

Plan calls (regardless of whether to specialists, handymen, customers, and so forth.) as soon as you can. Have every single fundamental material before you. Write down any key inquiries in advance so that you know what you want to say.

Make a not of every one of your activities. Everything that should be recollected should be jotted down somewhere. Notwithstanding when you have an gifted memory, no one is flawless, it wont hurt anyone to compose what you do on a piece of paper in the event of some unforeseen issue. Enlist telephone numbers, arrangements, birthday events, shopping records, and plan for the day.

Tips 8-14

In the event that you don't have room in your schedule to arrange a space from start to finish, start with the express form: evacuate just the messiness that is obvious to the eye. The space will feel more sorted out, inspiring you to handle whatever is left of it sooner rather than later.

Webster's characterizes mess as —a confounded large number of things‖. Check out the space you're cleaning up and look out for any things that look confused about where they are—i.e., have no point being there—making any piece of the space unusable.

Occurrences are things such as heaps of schoolwork on the kitchen counter, shoes strewn about, piles of old magazines, and so forth.

Simple Time Management

8.   Arrange documents.

Try not to sit idle searching for papers when you require them. Keep all printed material that relates to a specific task together in one major file. Among the most widely recognized approaches to organizing on your PC is as indicated by the date. Windows has numerous arranging capacities to organize your records, for example, by name, date, file type and size. Arranging your documents by date enables you to remain sorted out while having brief access to your most current records.

9.   Arrange time limits.

State, 'I have just 5 minutes to talk.' Outline your telephone calls, stating, 'I'd love to examine these 2 answers for issue A . . .'

Make a timetable. Record it on a bit of paper and stay with your timetable. While this may be the least demanding thing to do, it can be the hardest to stick to.

10. Create time for yourself.

Make no less than one screened meeting with yourself consistently. Screened time is peaceful, continuous time enabling you to focus on a task or get up to speed with your reading.

You'll figure out how to be straightforward in the amount you may achieve in a given time.

11. Delegate.

Understand that you can't do everything. Delegate in the workplace and at home. To use a successful appointment framework, you need to prepare, believe, develop and assess. Brief the person on the task: Define what he is in charge of. Clarify how the

task fits into the bigger venture. Illuminate goals and settle on finishing dates for it.

12.   Do not pack filing cabinets to the top.

There's nothing more awful than filing papers in a file organizer that is overrun! Leave sufficient room in drawers so you're not utilizing all your time to get a bit of paper in or out. Get rid of any paper you needn't bother with! Hurl out information you never again require. Reuse papers when you can. Do whatever it takes not to hold tight to magazines and lists.

13.   Have imaginary dates to finish by.

In the event that you've a due date toward the end of the month, keep in mind the due date 4 days sooner. You'll dispose of that last minute rush to finish the task as you'll have given yourself sufficient cushioning to get the work done.

Have a think over what may divert you from staying on track. The more time that is needed, the more urgent it is that you're sensible about what else is on your plate of things to get done. Characterize each subtask, and set begin and end dates for each of them. Constantly assess how practical your time allotment is. In case you're coming up short on time, at that point get innovative and start trimming errands.

14.   Utilize timekeepers and alarms.

Divide time for your everyday activities and exercises, from chipping away at activities to doing home tasks. At that point set clocks or any alarms to keep you on track. Set a PC alert to attract your thoughtfulness regarding an up and coming occasion or to wake you from a snooze.

Tips 15-21

Keep in mind that vision you made for the space you wish to sort out? In all probability, it excludes the messiness living there! Your following stage is to dispose of it. Every last bit of it.

Here comes the crucial step, basic decisions! An awesome thought for arranging is to take four vast canisters or boxes and name them, KEEP, SELL, DONATE and GARBAGE. The next step to advance in getting sorted out is to now sort out your stuff and place everything into one of these boxes that are labelled.

The start of being able to declutter is being able to do deal with it mentally. You need to decide that you're prepared to do it. It resembles some person starting a better eating routine; advising an individual not to eat doesn't help. An individual will just get in shape when they settle on a time to change the way they eat.

Cleaning up is the same. The physical exertion is to a lesser degree than the mental factor.

Time and Space

15.   Make awesome use of room.

Include racking for books and manuals. Include space extenders in work area drawers. Buy full-suspension file organizers. Use stacking bins and containers.

Choose furniture on account of capacity and space. When purchasing a couch, get one with a container underneath that is able to stow away materials. Buy beds for the children that have a dresser connected to it. Pick taller dressers and bookshelves.

Re-evaluate your choices. An empty space in a chest of drawers may hold toiletries and make up items you can't fit in the bathroom. Have a suitcase or holiday bag that you very rarely use? Why not store your bed sheets in it? Old handbags and purses can be used to store smaller clothing items such as socks. Bookshelves can in like manner hold knickknacks and smaller ornaments that you have collected over the years.

16. Make the most of down time.

Individuals lose a considerable measure of their time pausing and waiting. Waiting at a specialist's office, a transport stop or at an air terminal is ordinary. A considerable measure of people may see waiting time as the kind of time that is simply lost and not able to be retrieved ever again, yet waiting time doesn't need to be misused time.

You can really utilize this]time to complete a few things.

There are a ton of ways you can utilize this all the more beneficially. Make up for lost time with your reading while you sit tight for arrangements. Recordings or podcasts of an instructive or motivational nature are a fantastic method to gain extra knowledge while heading to work.

17. Get the kids off to their school day quicker.

The trick to mastering this is don't leave everything for the morning when everybody is in a rush. The night earlier, enable get your kids to select their outfits, choose what they wish to eat and figure out what they require for school. Pack snacks that night.

Beforehand, put the snacks into tinier plastic containers that are easy for them to get a hold of in the morning. Keep bread and their most loved sandwich stuff like flavored spreads and meats in there so when you make lunch you should simply grab the box of ingredients and every one of the provisions are there.

This will separate the lunch snacks and at home bites, so you won't be found napping when the provisions must be renewed.

18. Set up stopping time.

On the off chance that you need to work late, or amid the end of the week, set time limits for yourself. Regardless of whether you work for 2 or 4 hours, quit working toward the tail end of that time and appreciate whatever is left of the night or end of the week.

Plan your stopping time for every day, including ends of the week. My stopping time isn't genuinely a period of day, more along the lines of how long a day of work I will put in. Each day is different but make sure that you allocate a deadline for each day.

19.   Where does it belong?

Don't simply hurl your extra keys and different gadgets in a shoebox without first recognizing what they are. Mark each thing with a name of what it is. Names and labels are a critical piece of organizing. Using multi-use stickers/labels may decrease the time you put into naming things around your house. In spite of the fact that making these that you can use again and again will require some time, you'll spare time in the long run when you see how well they work. Like color coding certain categories with a specific color can make the items more easily identifiable.

20. Wipe out Wildfires.

These are quite often caused by being un-organized. Wipe out the disorder and you'll take out the wildfires. They may even devour a man's property. This is especially accurate if a house or vehicle is gobbled up by a wildfire, which may obliterate these things.

Regardless of whether individual property isn't totally devoured, the harm that wildfires may cause is much of the time sufficiently critical to require a lot of repairs (modifying, repainting, and so forth.).

These fires may in like manner demolish land, consuming grass and roasting trees. A major wildfire can transform a wonderful large area of land into a roasted fix of soil, making it useless till everything develops again.

21. Ascertain your most valuable time for any jobs that you may have to do.

Use your most profitable time to do your most gainful work.

Handle your hardest, critical work amid the point in the day when you're feeling your best and get it done, and you will be well on the way to completing it.

Tips 22-28

Try to spend just ten minutes per day on your physical mail, it won't get heaped up. Only aim to touch each bit of paper once. Also, don't open your mail without your planner at hand to make takes note of, your checkbook available, and a charge card close by.

Bills might be placed to be payed once every week. Solicitations might be put into your logbook and disposed of (or in case you're visual, posted on a message board till the date of the occasion), magazine subscriptions should be instantly disposed of (and withdraw from them – there's nothing you can't get online that is in that book you keep getting every week), and receipts may go into a little accordion type file that isolates them by month or subject.

Magazines that are being used should be set where they're probably going to be read (a night table or folder, to be read while driving to work). Newer issues of magazines and other reading material can be disposed of as the new ones come in.

Records and Planning

22.   Utilize control lists and daily agendas.

Assume responsibility of your time throughout the day. When used legitimately, these successful points will give you a particular thought of what you need to achieve. How frequently have you've gotten somewhere just to overlook what you required in the first place?

Note to self: Writing plans for the day spares time, vitality, and releases the pressure. An awesome rundown gives you a chance to forget, once you have a composed update, your cerebrum is allowed to focus on different things. A plan for the day even encourages you to meet your objectives. Regardless of whether you're a lawyer, a personal assistant or call center worker, pick a plan that works, note it down and use it!

23. Arrange firm due dates.

Setting a due date makes you progress in the direction of it. Set a distinct date and time. Expressing, 'When I get a chance' or 'At some point' is not good enough. Set your timetable for progress. Be particular with the coveted outcome.

Be sensible and kind to yourself. On the off chance that you wish to see yourself succeed, don't make a circumstance that only a hero may achieve. Set your goals, and work backwards step by step to produce a timeline of how long this is all going to take you.

Objectives like taking to learning another ability, weight reduction, and travelling to certain places you have always wanted to go to, may all be accomplished inside a time span.

Different objectives, similar to growing spiritually or developing of beneficial habits, may proceed for the duration of your life. With an objective, it serves to record particularly what advances you might want to accomplish inside a specific timeframe.

24. Use a Birthday/Anniversary planner.

Consider a separate folder/file to recall birthday events, commemorations and extra unique occasions. These resemble a small notepad, aside from that each page has a month to month section to hold birthday cards etc. You can pencil in birthday events, occasions, and so forth for consistency, furthermore, you can buy your cards all in one go beforehand!

25.   Design your garden early.

Start arranging your garden in the winter. Choose what you'll plant. Read up on the best possible care of your plants, blooms and vegetables.

Draw your garden out of how you want it to look like. Snatch a bit of paper and portray out your thoughts; your illustrations don't need to be works of art as long as they enable you to imagine your thoughts. On the off chance that you need something more detailed, plot your garden to scale on a bit of diagram paper. When spring arrives, you'll be set up to start developing it all.

26.   Stash away similar things together.

Classification is extremely significant when you're getting sorted out. Keep all bill paying supplies in a single place. Keep all of your bits and bobs for any hobbies in the same box. Keep your photographs in a single plastic container. Use cabinet dividers to keep any overflowing toy boxes or utensil drawers under wraps. Subsequent to separating off drawers into littler spaces, put similar things together for quicker access.

27. Categorize your documents.

To begin with, choose general classifications as per the particular work materials in your office. At that point, document one after another in order or sequentially inside these categories you have chosen.

Most people find that they wind up having a larger range of categories and it ends up noticeably overpowering. Marking by month implies you just have 12 to manage. Secondly, numerous costs and bills don't fit into one class. One single receipt from Target or

Wal-Mart may fit under household, wellbeing related buys or tax deductible expenses.

28.   Plan dinners.

Plan your dinners before you head out to do you food shopping. It will spare time, as you'll know exactly what you will require. Your dinners should:

1)   Be very much adjusted and nutritious

2) Provide combinations

3) Be inside your spending plan

4) Fit within your time limits

Plan what you will make with any leftovers from other meals. For example, in case you will cook a chicken, the extra chicken might be utilized to make a chicken soup.

On the off chance that you wish to make homemade burgers, buy additional meat to use in stews or tacos. Pick 2 or 3 fundamental dishes to make for the week. At the point when you can join with extras left over from other meals, you can then have made extra solid dinners anticipated for the entire week.

Tips 29-36

The measure of stuff an individual needs is a personal thing and depends on the life style you choose to live. As far as way of life, it would rely upon how much stuff you require. Do you have an alternate way of life for work and for the weekend? Do you go out a great deal during the evening? Do you like to go out shopping?

You need to consider how much wardrobe space and cabinet space you have. Over the long haul, your stuff will make you feel unhappy if it is that you have no place to put them. A good guideline to always follow is: don't buy more than you can store.

Choices

29. Put things away day by day.

Set aside opportunity to return things back to where they came from. Put them back immediately after you're done with them or set up a 15-minute slot at the end of the day to return things.

Make new tendencies for yourself by repeating particular activities daily at specific times. Being able to be disciplined will improve your life and raise your sense of pride. Numerous people wish to wind up noticeably more self-trained, yet genuinely don't know how to go about it. There are a ton of accommodating approaches to change your life through self-restraint.

30.   Remove any old reading material.

Go through your reading stack. Get rid of old newspapers. Dump magazines that have been lying around than three months. Keep just two or three items that you truly appreciate.

31.   Clear out your library.

Look through your shelves and give away books you've had for quite a while and will never take a gander at again. Foundations are continually looking for gifts to put towards their reading programs.

Giving books to a library is also advantageous. Unfortunately, most libraries can't keep the greater part of the books that they get by gift. A great deal of libraries have rules set up for what they may and may not take of your hands. Nonetheless, most bookkeepers know about a couple of associations that would be happy to get your given books.

32.   Draft in your colleagues.

Does your home need painting? A great method to take care of business rapidly is to arrange a work party. They supply the assistance. You supply the pizza, sandwiches, drinks and sweets. You likewise need to consider the conditions of the weather as you won't know what it is going to be like that far ahead of time so ensure you have a second date to do this on in case of any inconveniences.

33. Keep receipts together.

Keep up an envelope in your purse or wallet to hold receipts that you may requirement for cost records or expense purposes. When you return to your office or home, put the receipts in pre-assigned envelopes (business, gas, rental costs etc), at that point keep every one of the envelopes in a larger filing box.

Make a system for yourself for sorting out your receipts that best works for you. Have a go at arranging your receipts as indicated by date, sort of receipt or even one after another in order. Join those diverse approaches to sort out your receipts. Utilize experimentation to discover what works best for you and that will make your life easier.

34. Throw out old PC material.

Programming discs, CDs, PC manuals, et cetera for PC programs you never again use and never will again. PC producers stack a great deal of unneeded free or trial programming onto their PCs to influence you to believe you're getting a considerable amount more for your cash. You won't want or need a large portion of it.

Choose what you wish to do with your PC, at that point go to the "Control Panel" and uninstall any product that doesn't fit into your plans to utilize the PC. This will free up space and expel a great deal of messiness from the start up menu and folders that you regularly use. In case you're uncertain about any program, don't uninstall it without doing a little bit of research about what it is and if you do actually need it.

35.   Co-ordinate with other individuals.

Cooperate with other individuals, friends and family, or associates, to think of ideas that are straightforward and successful for everyone included.

Open up a meeting to generate new ideas. Have individuals begin saying their thoughts and this ought to be done rapidly. There's no time for discussing in depth this piece of the meeting to generate new ideas. Put down ALL thoughts, All thoughts, whether they sound brilliant at first or not, must be noted down. Then afterwards you can go through any ideas you have relating to your topic in more depth once everyone has given their own initial input.

36. Utilize a work space organizer.

Keep an adequate supply of pens, pencils, paperclips, scissors and extra important supplies in a work area holder around your work area for efficiency and speed.

Tips 37-43

There are a couple of things that are intended to be put away and may not have been taken out or looked at lately, such as gifts, nostalgic letters or pictures, for example. However. these things should be spared.

Other than that, unless something is being put aside for a specific reason (if a certain piece of equipment was expensive but you use it a couple of times a year), you should dispose of what you haven't used or looked at in over a year. It's an extremely awesome, dependable guideline.

Being Ahead of The Game

37.   Produce a decent working area.

Create a lovely, all around prepared work place. Regardless of whether it's a small corner or a major office, your work territory should be helpful to completing your everyday work. It should contain every fundamental supply you need inside arms reach or in effectively accessible places.

Take a look around. Be straightforward, would you welcome in customers, or would you bolt the door shut? Evaluate what should be finished. Do you need to reposition the work area? Paint the walls? Get rid of any mess? Scribble down any problem areas that you wish to address and write out a shopping list in the event that you to require a couple of things.

38.   Magnetize your medication chest.

Mount a long magnet along the back of your cabinet or drawer to hold tweezers, scissors, little scissors and extra little metal items.

Throw away the things you don't use anymore or that are excessively old. Likely pieces good for the trash are old toothbrushes (which should be changed every 3 months), old sunscreens (useful for just a single year after buy), gunky nail lacquer, out of date over-the-counter cures (pills, creams and moisturizers), and out of date solutions or medications that you never use.

39.   Rest and loosen up.

Get an extraordinary night's rest (7 hours or all the more.) Enough rest around evening time will help you to be cautious, on plan and powerful the morning after. Keep yesterdays worries behind you. Endeavor to take two or three full breaths and let yourself relax and take everything in for a short time. This is your opportunity to recover for the day ahead. Try not to let any worries from today stop you from being ready for the next day.

40.   Make moving houses simple.

A good way to do this is to color code your boxes and cases with a sticky yellow spot for those that go to the kitchen, a red one for the workplace, a blue one for the carport etc. Go to your new home beforehand and place a comparing shaded speck on the suitable rooms so that unpacking is made just that little bit easier and you don't have to start looking through everything as soon as you get to your new place.

41.   Fix any mail beforehand.

In the event that you send similar booklets and different materials to clients, make your bundles previously before the actual day that they are to go out. Incorporate every single important material and store them away till you require them. They'll be all prepared to go in a snap.

42.   Produce reference records.

Reference records are incredible for recalling and getting to everything effortlessly.

Make these reference records for:

- Personal objectives and desires

- Birthdays

- Restaurant phone numbers

- Internet sites that are your favorite or you use regularly

- Books you'd get a kick out of reading

- Things to pack while going on vacation

- Gift thoughts for colleagues and friends and family

- PC files

- A list of things to get for yourself

- And more. Your choices are endless!

Change the shade of pen or text style on the PC you use for each of these. This will enable your things to stand out from the normal typography you are used to seeing, and it will likewise enable you to recall what you have to complete for the duration of the day on the off chance that you're not close to your physical list.

43. Produce structures for every day jobs.

For example, type up your own Transmittal sheet that includes things such as your name, company name, email address, contact number and any other information you wish to include. Make copies of them and leave them close to your desk.

Create a document in Excel, which will deliver straightforward content fields where the client may enter their data. Make 3 integrated command buttons that will affect the data in the shape when the client left-clicks with their mouse for example.

It's anything but difficult to create a document that will list workers or directors and check their status.

Tips 44-50

Your clean up sessions need to end with a place being assigned for each little thing and piece of paper that comes into your home or office.

As you would commit a certain amount of time to your exercise or eating routine, you have to burn through ten minutes daily placing everything into its place.

Unfortunately, there is a consistent attack of new messages, lists, phone calls, and consumerism that enter our lives on an everyday premise. On the off chance that you don't keep on top of it, it's only normal for all of this to build up.

It will be dependent upon only you to keep up with this.

De-Stress It

44.   Produce a directions folder.

Create a record for Driving Directions to places you go to rarely. Put down the headings and keep them in this folder for future usage. You won't need to continue requesting how get to where you're going.

Print each stage of your journey from a site like MapQuest or Google Maps. In spite of how popular these sites may be, every so often they can contain incorrect, obsolete or deficient data. It's great to have these bearings, however, as regardless of whether they instruct you to turn down a wrong street, you will always have the version that you have created for yourself prior which you know you can trust if your sat nav tells you otherwise.

45.   Provide driving directions to your place of work.

Create a list of directions to your home or office, originating from North, South, East and West. Make duplicates and keep in a record. When someone asks, you can mail them, fax them or read them via telephone. Name changeless historic points, similar to stoplights, monuments and railroad tracks.

Be excess ' give road names alongside historic landmarks.

Add notices, name puts things that will be seen along the way if they happen to travel too far so they know to turn around or not.

Consider giving distances between any roads or buildings. Include your contact number with the directions just incase they happen to get lost and need your help and guidance.

46.   Decide to what extent it will take.

Figure to what extent it will take to arrive. Divide your total amount of miles for the excursion, by your normal speed (e.g. 60mph) the result will be your total driving time. (for example: a one hundred and twenty miles journey divided by sixty mph is around two hours of driving time).

Add time to gauge for stops. Consider how many times you will need to eat whilst travelling. Dinners will take around half-hour for most people, and considerably more in the event that you have a larger family.

Remember that you may need to make a stop for gas, dinners, restroom breaks and any other reasons that may arise.

47. Cut back on the amount of junk mail.

Expelling yourself from junk mail is the most ideal approach to eliminate the measure of garbage mail that comes in your post box and email inbox consistently. All of that waste paper from too much junk mail takes its toll on the environment, and junk emails only take up space and create limit issues that may create disturbances in sending and receiving new emails.

48. Merge your time.

With expanding requests on our lives, our work lives, feared housekeeping, raising our families, discovering time for exercise so important for good wellbeing, correspondence through phones, texts or emails, we oftentimes end up dashing around against the clock. To adjust, multi-tasking is a lifestyle for a large number of us who are searching for ways to help to spare time and be more profitable in our day by day routines. The amount of technology that is available to us that lets us multi-task at work, in the car, at home, and at numerous different places and events.

We find ourselves multi-tasking with assignments we never figured we could do in the same time. Search for things you can join together to spare time and accomplish more. Walk your dog and you'll be combining exercise at the same time. Go to the beach or park with a motivational audio book and you will be in a relaxing environment whilst getting motivated at the same time!

49. Finish each day on an incredible note.

Spare your most straightforward tasks for the finish line of every day. You'll easily be able to complete them and end each day on a positive! Look on the good side. You don't need to give these little irritations a chance to demolish a generally awesome day. In case you're stuck in rush hour gridlock, use this opportunity to complete that audio book you were listening to.

50.   Continually grow.

Preparing and training your organization skills is always ongoing. With new procedures and frameworks popping up every day inside PC programs and cell phones, the training never stops.

Associating yourself with organizing abilities makes business and day by day tasks more proficient and effective.

Conclusion

Here are a couple of the advantages you can hope to procure from getting yourself organized:

- Save time — you never again search for similar things over and over or need to replace all of those things you can't discover no matter how hard you look.

- Save money at work — on the off chance that you pay a supervisor $75,000 every year, and that individual squanders an hour daily searching for lost material, that expenses to $9,000 every year. Moreover, it's difficult to put a price on incomplete tasks or lost opportunities.

- Save money at home — when you realize what you have and where it is, you won't squander money acquiring similar things once more. When you cut down your amount of possessions, you can quit paying for storage units from month to month. You may decide to hold a yard sale and make a little money in the process, or you may donate to charities.

- Cut down pressure and stress — when you know where everything is, there's no last minute rush to discover what you require and get out the front door on schedule for school, sports practice, or that business conference.

- Be more productive — all the time you once spent searching for things may now be utilized to accomplish more essential or more enjoyable tasks throughout the day.

- Move ahead — perhaps you feel caught in the past by years of aggregated mess. Or on the other hand possibly a separation or loss in the family has left you with more things on your hands than you know what to do with. Dealing with your property and any paperwork with a professional organizer who may give direction and comprehension, may enable you to get through a deadlock and start advancing once more.

- Feel certain — when you get your spaces well-kept once more, you will feel pride in your accomplishment. Also, you're assuring yourself that you'll have the capacity to keep up your new organizing system.

- Gain opportunity — When mess no longer controls you, you can pick how you invest your energy and how your home or office looks. Your life feels like yours again.

Thanks again for buying my book. If you have a minute, please leave a positive review. You can leave your review by clicking on this link:

Leave your review here. Thank you!

I take reviews seriously and always look at them. This way, you are helping me provide you better content that you will LOVE in the future. A review doesn't have to be long, just one or two sentences and a number of stars you find appropriate (hopefully 5 of course).

Also, if I think your review is useful, I will mark it as "helpful." This will help you become more known on Amazon as a decent reviewer, and will ensure that more authors will contact you with free e-books in the future. This is how we can help each other.

DISCLAIMER: This information is provided "as is." The author, publishers and/or marketers of this information disclaim any loss or liability, either directly or indirectly as a consequence of applying the information presented herein, or in regard to the use and application of said information. No guarantee is given, either expressed or implied, in regard to the merchantability, accuracy, or acceptability of the information. The pages within this e-book have been copyrighted.

Printed in Great Britain
by Amazon